Psychotherapy for Families:
Facilitating Systemic Change

Books in This Series

Crisis Intervention for Community Behavioral Health Service Providers in Ohio

Overcoming Reluctance in Therapeutic Relationships

Psychotherapy for Families

Therapeutic Behavioral Services Using Interventions Based on Principles and Techniques of Cognitive Behavioral Therapy

Treating Attention Deficit Hyperactivity Disorder, Impulsivity, and Disruptive Behaviors in Children Using Behavioral Skill Building and Cognitive Behavioral Therapy Skills and Interventions

Treating Anxiety Using Cognitive Behavioral Therapy Skills and Interventions

Treating Depression Using Cognitive Behavioral Therapy Skills and Interventions

Treating Posttraumatic Stress Disorder Using Cognitive Behavioral Therapy Skills and Interventions

Psychotherapy for Families:
Facilitating Systemic Change

INTERVENTION MANUAL

Reinhild Boehme, LISW-S

Benjamin Kearney, PhD, *series editor*

THE INSTITUTE OF
FAMILY & COMMUNITY IMPACT

An OhioGuidestone Company
Berea, Ohio

Nothing contained in the manual is, or should be considered or used as, a substitute for medical advice, diagnosis, or treatment. The manual is not intended to replace, and does not replace, the specialized training and professional judgment of a health care or mental health care professional. Individuals should seek the advice of a physician or other health care provider with any questions regarding medications, personal health or medical conditions. This manual has been prepared as a tool to assist providers. In its efforts to provide information that is accurate and generally in accord with the standards of practice at the time of publication, the author has checked with sources believed to be reliable. However, in view of the possibility of human error or changes in behavioral, mental health, or medical sciences, neither the author, nor the editor and publisher, nor any other party who has been involved in the preparation or publication of this work warrants that the information contained herein is in every respect accurate or complete, and they are not responsible for any errors or omissions, or the results obtained from the use of such information. Further, the information presented in this manual does not constitute legal or financial advice or opinions. The ultimate responsibility for correct billing lies with the provider of the services. The reader should consult the current version of the relevant laws, regulations, and rulings.

The Institute of Family and Community Impact
An OhioGuidestone Company
www.OhioGuidestone.org

ISBN 978-1-7328190-4-7
Printed in the United States of America

Contents

Preface

For mental health professionals, building trusting relationships with clients and knowing which interventions will most benefit them are challenging enough. Helping clients who are also dealing at the same time with chronic conditions such as poverty, violence, and addiction can seem overwhelming. That's especially true for behavioral health service providers who have limited experience. That's why we at OhioGuidestone have developed this series of clinical manuals to help professionals develop their skills while providing effective treatment.

OhioGuidestone, the largest community behavioral health organization in Ohio, regularly trains new therapists and other behavioral health interventionists to work with clients who face severe, therapy-interfering challenges. We've brought that experience to these manuals.

In this era of managed care oversight, tight funding, and pressure to deliver evidence-based or informed care, it is essential for new therapists to get up to speed on best practices quickly. It is also essential for experienced clinicians to be well provided with effective and varied treatment plans. The manuals in this series provide step-by-step guidance on evidence-based and informed treatment modalities and interventions that can be used by both licensed and unlicensed mental health professionals—as well as by their supervisors for training purposes.

Seasoned mental health professionals will find the resources offered in these manuals useful for developing a renewed focus on evidence- and research-based interventions. At OhioGuidestone, our interventions are grounded in cognitive behavioral science and also shaped by the relational and attachment scientific advances that continue to inform the behavioral health field (especially the interpersonal neurobiology work published by W. W. Norton & Company). We understand the demands of serving client populations experiencing trauma and toxic stress. Our interventions are designed not to address discrete diagnoses (clients often have more than one) but rather the symptoms that are related to them. The series addresses a wide range of issues, such as depression, anxiety, ADHD, PTSD, and even reluctance to engage in therapy, and it provides interventions for children and adults.

We cannot "fix" our clients. But we can guide them along clear paths toward developing the skills they need to navigate the challenges they face, in their thoughts and in their lives. It's our sincere hope that the books in this series will help better prepare more mental health professionals to do just that.

— Benjamin Kearney, PhD, series editor

If you purchased this manual and want to make copies of interventions to help your clients, please do so. However, please do not share copies with other professionals but encourage them to buy manuals for themselves. This will help us continue to add to and update this series, to better equip all helpers who make a difference.

What is Psychotherapy for Families?

Psychotherapy for families is different from individual therapy because treatment is focused on family dynamics and how they relate to client symptoms and problems. Treatment is focused on systemic problems rather than just individual problems and symptoms with the understanding that systemic problems affect all parts of the system, including your client. When providing psychotherapy for families, keep in mind that treatment:

- is focused on the family system;

- addresses relationships, conflict, and communication;

- examines family processes, roles, hierarchies, intergenerational patterns, culture;

- can use "in vivo" interventions to practice skills and build insight.

To further develop your understanding of family therapy concepts, you may want to read *Family Therapy: Concepts and Methods*, by M.P. Nichols and S. D. Davis (2017, Pearson).

The session includes family members, guardians, and/or significant others, and can be provided with or without the client present. Examples:

- Therapist meets with Sam's parents, and works to build insight around the cycles of Sam's tantrums and the impact on the family and how to intervene in a trauma-sensitive way.

- Johnny's anxiety is causing an increase in irritability and family communication is strained. He and his parents are working on communication techniques in a family session.

- Beth has been getting into frequent conflicts with her parents and significant other. A family session is held to work on conflict resolution.

What If a Family Member/Collateral Is Present, But We Are Not Working on Family Dynamics?

This would simply be psychotherapy. The client must be present for all or a majority of the service, and treatment is focused on the client's individual symptoms and problems. Examples:

- Therapist checks in with Sam's parent to monitor symptoms for 10 minutes, then spends 50 minutes working on trauma narrative with Sam.

- Johnny's parents are in the session learning about his cognitive distortions and how to help him reframe his thinking.

- Beth's partner is in her session, learning about her symptoms of depression and how it affects her daily functioning.

Family Work: Helpful Assumptions

1. People generally mean well. But hurt people will hurt people, often unintentionally. Because of this, begin with compassion. You are modeling a new way of relating.
2. Change is possible.
3. Change can be difficult: Make the work as joyful as it can be. Be creative.
4. Motivation for change is built during interactions. It is not a prerequisite for change.
5. Change in one family member can effect change in other family members. Families work as a system.
6. Parents and caretakers are your go-to change agents. They are a part of the family every day, and probably have the greatest capacity to make changes. Work hard to build alliances with them.
7. Make sure all family members get a chance to explain what changes they need. You are trying to get everyone on board as much as possible.
8. Pay attention to scapegoating in the family. If you see it, there is probably an important family issue behind it to address.
9. Give voice to the "weak" in the family. They often have important things to say. Help family members recognize the contributions each of them makes to the family.
10. Frequently, those who are not present are important for understanding family dynamics. Ask about those who are not there, but who "show up" anyway (such as the abusive, alcoholic grandfather or the incarcerated sibling).
11. Some family members will need individualized support and services. Refer them for the appropriate services to support the family work.

Trauma Informed Care, Toxic Stress, and Psychotherapy for Families

Clients in the community mental health setting tend to have been exposed to adverse childhood experiences (ACEs) at high rates. In fiscal year 2016–2017, 55% of OhioGuidestone clients surveyed had an ACEs score of four or more. Therefore, it is important to incorporate principles of trauma informed care into the provision of services, including psychotherapy for families. When working with families, remember that:

- The family as a whole may be exposed to ongoing experiences of toxic stress.

- Intergenerational trauma may express itself in family interactions.

- Many clients experience toxic stress in the form of discrimination and marginalization.

- We must acknowledge power differentials and work to create a safe therapeutic environment.

- Trauma and toxic stress may have contributed to or created systemic family problems.

- Trauma and toxic stress can reset the stress response system, and some or all family members may be in survival mode. In survival mode, the fight/flight response is triggered easily, which can lead to problems in family interactions and in the ways the family interacts with "outsiders."

- Building safety within the therapeutic relationship for those exposed to trauma and toxic stress takes time and conscious effort.

- Cultural competence requires you to develop a stance of humble inquisitiveness.

On Genograms

Genograms have become a widespread tool in the provision of family therapy. Murray Bowen was the first to recognize the "mapping" of families as a critical tool for family assessment and intervention. Genograms are now used widely in many schools of family therapy, as well as in child welfare institutions. Monica McGoldrick (2011) continues to explore and expand the use of genograms in family therapy, now incorporating cultural considerations and issues of marginalization and discrimination.

What Exactly Is a Genogram?

A genogram is a family map, a visual representation of all family members and their relationships, preferably incorporating three generations. Genograms often expand while you are working with the family. Over time, the family may be more willing to tell you about a "lost" uncle (who really is incarcerated) or the alcoholic and abusive grandfather (who is safely stored away in a nursing home).

What Can a Genogram Tell Me and the Family?

A genogram can help you and the family recognize a great deal, such as:

- quality of relationships;
- patterns in quality of relationships;
- intergenerational patterns of mental illness, addiction, and abuse/neglect;
- "lost" family members;
- isolation from family of origin;
- trauma or traumatic losses;
- relational wishes;
- fears and hopes for children that relate to other family members.

You can use a genogram when you are working on Part 2 of your Diagnostic Evaluation. You can also start a genogram when the family you are working with does not see its own dynamics. A genogram can really bring a systemic and intergenerational problem to light. You (and the family) can *see* the problem.

What Do Genograms Look Like?

Over the past few decades, genogram symbols have expanded greatly. Here are the basics:

☐ Male
◯ Female

- Family members can be connected by marriage by a line: _______________.
- A segmented line signifies that partners are living together, but are not married _ _ _ _ _ _.
- Death is signified by an X through the circle or square. The date of death is noted outside of the symbol.
- A diagonal line through a line signifying marriage indicates a separation, and two diagonal lines indicate a divorce.
- Ages of family members are indicated within their squares or circles.
- Children are listed in birth order, left to right.
- A pregnancy is indicated by a triangle. Miscarriages and abortions are indicated in the same way, but marked with an x. A stillbirth is indicated by a smaller circle or square with an x through it.

Here are the basic symbols for relational quality and problems:

◯----◯ Distant

☐〜〜◯ Hostile

☐—|—☐ Cutoff

☐〜〜▶◯ Sexual Abuse

☐〜〜▶◯ Physical Abuse

☐——☐ Close

☐===☐ Fused/too close/enmeshed

For more information about genogram symbols, refer to the Multicultural Family Institute's standard symbols for genograms, which can be found at this website: http://multiculturalfamily.org/

Is It Important to Use the "Proper" Genogram Symbols?

Using established genogram symbols can be helpful when you are using a genogram to communicate with an outside agency, such as a child welfare organization. When you are creating a genogram for and with your family, you can use established symbols and those that you create. Just make a note of what your invented symbols mean at the bottom of the page.

As families are constantly changing, so are genograms and their symbols. When genograms were invented, there was little awareness of issues of power, gender, race, and culture. In our work in community mental health, we need to sensitively and competently work those issues into our genograms. If we do not, we simply miss the mark. The genogram may look proper, but it may lack the information we need to discern family strengths, patterns, and problems. Family problems can originate within the family, or they can "migrate" in and shape it, as can be the case when a family is affected by decades of poverty and/or racism.

What is important is that you create a meaningful family map, one that helps everyone explore and understand how the family works and has worked. This can then be used to "map out" treatment needs. Here are some examples:

- Perhaps addiction has been a part of every generation, and a parent wants to break this cycle for a child.

- Perhaps hostile relationships are the norm, and the family is tired of this.

- Perhaps a mother who cut off the relationship with her mother fears that her daughter will do the same to her.

How Can I Make a Genogram Fun to Create?

- You can incorporate all kinds of interesting elements. Ask family members to choose animals to represent them in the genogram, and then ask about the characteristics of the animals.

- Ask family members to choose or make up songs to signify their positions in the family.

- Create a genogram board game.

- Create a "wishful genogram" in which relationships are depicted in the way people want them to be, as opposed to the way they are.

Keep in mind that a genogram is not something to "get done," but rather a creative tool for discovery and intervention. Ask poignant questions and listen carefully to the answers. The family genogram is a work in progress. It does not have to look tidy, but it should be decipherable.

Engage your family in creative ways when working on a genogram.

- It's OK to create your own symbols as long as you have a key at the bottom of the page to decode your genogram.

- Family members can feel more empowered if they create unique symbols.

- Families can incorporate systemic struggles, such as toxic stress, in their own way.

Interventions

INTERVENTION 1

Balancing Balloons

Balancing balloons asks family members to work together.

You will need: Several inflated balloons (family members may want to do this). Space to move about. Music in the background.

Target behaviors/emotions: Communication, collaboration, attunement.

1. Begin by sitting with all family members. Explain that you will ask them to balance a balloon together. Two people will hold a balloon up using their noses.

2. In order for this to work, you will need to match up participants by size. If you are working with a child, a parent may want to get on their knees to match size.

3. Once the balloon is firmly in place between noses, the partners (and there may be several sets) should gently start to move around to the music, but not too fast, as the balloon will fall.

4. Demonstrate this with a volunteer.

5. Explain that the goal is to keep the balloon up between the noses. If the balloon falls, just give it another try.

6. Explain that this is not a competition. No bumping into each other. This is about learning to work together.

7. Now, ask your family to engage in the exercise. Observe: How are people working together? What is difficult? Is there competition? Are parents/caretakers helpful? Is anyone bossy?

8. Let the exercise last at least three minutes, longer, if possible.

9. Ask everyone to sit down and reflect on the following questions, going around in a circle:

    - *What part of this was enjoyable?*

    - *What part was not?*

    - *How did you communicate with your partner?*

    - *What went wrong?*

    - *How did your partner help you? How did you help your partner?*

    - *If you became angry during this exercise, what did you say and do about it?*

10. Help all family members relate their answers to family struggles. Ask:

    - *How do we experience joy together?*

    - *What happens when we are upset?*

    - *How do we talk to each other, and how does the way we talk to each other help us or hurt us?*

- *What do we do when things go wrong? How does this affect* [name of the client]*?*

- *How do we help each other in this family? How can* [name of the client] *ask for help?*

- *How do we deal with anger? How does this affect* [name of the client]*?*

- *What can we do to work together "to keep the balloon in the air" to benefit both* [name of the client] *and the family?*

11. Assign homework: Ask each family member to pick a partner (make sure your client has one). Leave some balloons and ask the pairs to play "balance the balloon" together at least once. Explain again that this assignment is about working and having fun together. Give all family members a note card and ask them to write or draw on the card how they felt about each other after the assignment.

Animal Cards Bingo

Animal Cards Bingo asks all family members to compare themselves to the animal on the card they turned over and explore:

- In what way are they like this animal in the family?

- In what way are they not?

Example: Let's say you turn over a hedgehog card. You could say: "I am like a hedgehog because when dad is angry, I put out my sharp pins and roll up in a ball. I do this by saying something mean, and then I run into my room and slam the door."

You will need: Animal Card Bingo game. You can make this yourself by printing animal images. This has the advantage of being able to pick animals that may work well for this, such as hedgehog, giraffe, whale, chicken, hummingbird, pig, crab, pit bull, etc.

Target behaviors/emotions: Relational difficulties: withdrawal, aggression, anxious interactions.

1. Ask everyone to sit together at a table or on the floor.

2. Explain that you will be using Animal Bingo to explore how everyone in the family relates to each other.

3. Lay the cards out, face down. You may want to begin to model what can be said about animals and relationships.

4. Turn over the first card, then the second. If they do not match, you get to pick one of the two animals, then explore: In what way am I like this animal in the family? In what way am I not?

5. Model how to say meaningful things that explore relationships. Let's say you pick the pit bull. You could say: *Sometimes I feel like I am barking at you. But then I am not like the pit bull. I don't bite. I am all about helping, not hurting.*

6. If you match your cards, you get to keep them.

7. Now, go around. If people need help with this, especially children, help them find the words. But don't help too quickly. Give family members time to find the words.

8. Help everyone understand that they can only talk about themselves, not others, while playing Animal Bingo. Now is not the time to call grandpa a pit bull.

9. Once all the cards are gone, ask everyone to look at their cards and pick one.

10. Then ask them to explore again:

    - In what way am I like this animal in the family?

    - In what way am I not?

- Why do I like this animal so much? Is there a quality that this animal has that I would like to adopt?

11. Assign homework: Ask family members to practice the positive qualities of the animals they like in their interactions over the next week. If someone picked a Labrador and likes it because it is so cuddly, in what way could that person be comforting to themselves and to others in the family?

All Hands

All Hands asks family members to trace their hands, then create a work of art connecting those hands. There are elements of reflecting on both "me" and "us" in this intervention.

Target behaviors/emotions: Making connections, recognizing self as separate, yet connected. Valuing family and self.

You will need: Paper and drawing materials such as crayons, markers, colored pencils. Tape. Scissors.

1. Invite all family members to trace a hand. You may want to demonstrate. Remember: Younger children may need help with this. How family members help, don't help, or take over can provide important clinical information for you.

2. Ask family members to decorate their hand tracings. Say: *This is not about being very neat or artistic. Just make your hand say something important about you.* Give about 15–20 minutes for this. How long this takes depends on the family. You can tell those who are done that it is OK to doodle while waiting.

3. Once everyone is done, sit in a circle and ask each family member show their hand and explore the way in which they decorated their hand. Ask: *What does this hand say about you?*

4. When everyone has contributed, challenge the family to create a circle of hands. Make sure that everyone gets a turn with connecting the paper hands. Pay attention where each person's hand goes.

5. When the hands are all connected into a circle, say: *This is a picture of your family connected. You are all different. But together you form this beautiful circle.*

6. Sit together and explore with all present:

   - How different are these hands?
   - Are there some that look alike? If they do, in what way?
   - How do you feel about being "all stuck together"?
   - When is sticking together a good thing?
   - When is it not?
   - How do you handle togetherness in this family?
   - How do you handle difference?
   - How can you connect, even in tough times?

7. Assign homework: Give all family members index cards and ask them to write or draw about their need for connection as well as for independence.

INTERVENTION 4

Footprints

This intervention involves making individual footprints, one person after another, walking in a circle. These footprints will soon begin to overlap, creating an opportunity to explore individuality and connection within the family. You can also ask poignant questions, such as: What happens when you step on each other's toes?

You will need: A very large piece of paper. Water colors and large brushes. Towels and soap. Bucket of warm water. Several washcloths.

Target behaviors/emotions: Insight about self, need for individuality as well as connection, boundaries, conflict resolution.

1. Invite the family you are working with to make footprints together. Explain that this will involve removing socks and putting water colors on the bottoms of their feet.

2. Lay out the large piece of paper. Take off your socks and demonstrate how to make footprints by walking in a small circle on the large piece of paper (you do not need watercolor paint on your feet to demonstrate).

3. Ask for a volunteer to start. Ask for another volunteer to paint this person's foot with watercolor (they get to choose the color) and then ask them to quickly step on the paper and walk in a small circle (the way you did) making footprints. The painting of feet needs to take place right next to the paper. This will make it easier to contain any messes.

4. Once the volunteer has finished their footprints, they should step off the paper, sit and use a washcloth and warm water from the bucket to clean their feet.

5. Then keep going with making footprints until all family members have participated.

6. Children may enjoy this so much that they will hop or not walk in a perfect circle. This is OK.

7. Once everyone has created their footprints and cleaned up, sit together in a circle and take a look at what you see together. Help all family members reflect on what they have done together and what they see by asking:

   - *What did you see after the first person made their footprints?*

   - *What happened when the second person made their prints? Did prints begin to overlap?*

   - *After everyone made their footprints, what did the image look like? Colorful? Messy?*

   - *Was it fun to make footprints? Or did it feel too messy?*

8. Now, help them reflect on the "family footprint." Say:

> *In families, we still each have our own unique footprint, but when we all walk together, footprints begin to overlap. This means things can look messy, but at the same time, a whole new picture can emerge.*

Ask all family members to take a look at the family footprint as a whole. Ask:

- *How do you feel about this family footprint picture? Do you find it beautiful?*

- *Can you still see your footprint? Or is it all covered up?*

- *What is it like to be an individual in your family?*

- *Do you feel different when you are with your family than when you are alone? And if you do, how?*

- *Do you ever feel that your footprint is getting lost? Like others do not see you anymore?*

- *Are there times when it feels good to be a part of the larger group?*

- *Do you ever feel trampled on? Do you ever trample on others?*

- *How do you get to be yourself in this family?*

- *How do you connect with others in the family?*

9. Finish by saying:

> *Family can be a wonderful thing. Family can protect and comfort us. At other times, we can feel trampled on and forgotten. It is important to both connect and respect each other's need for being themselves.*

10. Assign homework: Give the family footprint image to the family. Ask them to write or draw important thoughts and feelings on the image over the next week. There are some rules about this, of course—no insults allowed, only "I" statements.

Hands On

This intervention will involve gentle touch (hand massage). Hence, it is important to determine if your family is ready for this. This is also a good time to teach your family about consent and boundaries. Some people do not like to be touched, for whatever reason. If this is the case, use this opportunity to help family members learn how to respect each other's physical boundaries.

You will need: Massage oil. Simple vegetable oil will do.

Target behaviors/emotions: Asking for, accepting, and giving comfort. Accepting and communicating about boundaries.

1. Sit in a circle or around a table and welcome everyone.

2. Explain that, today, you will explore what it feels like to ask for, give, and receive comfort in the form of a hand massage.

3. Explain right away that part of today's exercise is to learn to say "no," if the hand massage is unwanted for any reason, and to accept the "no" from others. Explain that no justification is needed for not wanting a hand massage. It's OK to say "no."

4. Ask for a volunteer to demonstrate a gentle hand massage. Sit opposite each other. Ask: *May I touch your hand?* If the person agrees, use just a dab of oil and demonstrate how to gently massage a hand. Emphasize the "gentle" part. The massage should last a few minutes. Intermittently ask for feedback. Once you are done, say: *We are now done.*

5. Ask everyone to find a partner—or, if necessary, assign partners—and sit opposite each other. Explain the following steps:

   - Ask: *Can I touch your hand?*

   - If the answer is *yes*, give a gentle hand massage.

   - Ask for feedback once or twice and adjust what you are doing, as needed.

   - If someone does not want to be touched, ask: Is another way that I can give you comfort? Perhaps you want to listen to some music together on the phone. Or you could look at a beautiful image together for the duration of this exercise.

   - Make sure to take turns.

6. Once everyone has taken a turn, help them reflect on the exercise, using the following questions:

   - *How do you comfort each other in this family?*

   - *Is it OK to ask for comfort in this family?*

   - *How do you approach each other? How is touch handled? Do you ask each other: Can I have a hug? Or do you just hug?*

- *What happens in your family if someone does not want to be touched? Is this OK? Do they have to explain why?*

- *How do you communicate about boundaries?*

- *How are boundary violations handled?*

7. Assign homework: Ask the pairs who worked together to engage in one comforting activity together in the following week. It can be hand massage, but it does not have to be. If a pair did not work well together, you may have to do some reshuffling.

Going to Town

The family you are working with will create a "town map." If their family were a town, what would it look like?

You will need: A very large piece of paper (you can tape together printer paper). Tape. Drawing materials. Scissors. Old magazines and glue.

Target behaviors/emotions: Creating connections, building bridges, creating safety, collaboration.

1. Invite the family to think of themselves as a town. Explain that towns have common elements: bridges, roads, post offices, houses, police and fire departments, etc.

2. Explain that in order for a town to work, many of these elements have to be there. If there is no fire department, the town is really not safe. If there are no bridges, people can't get to each other.

3. Invite the family to begin creating their town. Each family member should begin by drawing a house for themselves. Remind everyone that this activity is not about perfection. It is OK to be creative! A house can be round, or a tower, or underground—whatever kind of dwelling they want. Give everyone at least 10 minutes to draw.

4. Once the houses are created, ask: What is missing? Make a list of what is missing (such as bridges, roads, etc.). Then ask each family member to pick one item from the list and draw it. Note that when talking about roads, they should be drawn one by one. Family members should take turns drawing roads. So perhaps grandma will draw a road from her house to your client's house, and vice versa. Next, your client can draw a road where he wants to.

5. Once everyone has drawn their extra item, take a look at the town now. Check to see if there is anything else missing. Create another list and have each family member pick another item. (You could keep this intervention going for more than one session, if needed.)

6. Once the town map is complete, take a look together and reflect on the following questions:

   - How similar are the houses?
   - How close together or far apart are they? Does proximity suggest anything about family relationships? If houses are far apart, does this mean anything?
   - If this were a real town, would you want to live there? Why? Or why not?
   - Is this town safe? If not, what could make it safe?
   - Is there a place to have fun?

- If someone is sad in this town, where do they go? Who do they visit?
- What needs repair? What needs rebuilding?

7. Help all present to reflect on ways in which their family is like the town they created.

8. Assign homework: Ask each family member to draw something that needs to be added to the town.

9. Explain that you will store the map and the family can add to it.

INTERVENTION 7

What I Need from You

This intervention encourages family members in a playful way to express needs. Because this can be difficult in families, a template is provided in the form of individual needs written out on popsicle sticks. Family members draw the sticks from a can.

You will need: Popsicle sticks or tongue depressors, each labeled with a need, such as:

- Love
- Compassion
- Attention
- Support
- Kindness
- Caring
- Affection
- Time
- Listening
- Playfulness
- Quiet Companionship
- Alone Time
- Forgiveness

The sticks are best stored in a container with a lid, so you can reuse them. You could do this with paper strips, but those often get lost or destroyed.

Target Behavior/Emotions: Communication, recognizing needs, getting needs met.

1. Welcome everyone and explain that, today, you will explore what people in families may need from each other. Ask everyone to sit in a circle.

2. Introduce the activity. Say:

   We will go around picking sticks from this can. Each stick contains a human need written on it. Once you pick your stick, read aloud what it says. Then, pick a person in your family to tell about this need.

3. Sometimes important family members cannot be present. If someone picks an absent family member, this is OK. Provide an empty chair and ask that person to direct their need to that chair.

4. Explain that the other person's role is to listen, not to judge. Once the need is explained, the listener should restate the need and ask: "Did I get this right?" If a family member is talking to an empty chair, ask for a volunteer to play the role of the absent person.

5. Explain that the aim is to fully understand what the other person needs. While the first family member expresses a need to the other family member, the entire family must also listen without interrupting the speaker. Everyone in the family should listen until it is clear that the other person got it right.

6. You then move to the next person, drawing a stick, and so forth.

7. Pay attention to who meets needs in the family and who has urgent, unmet needs.

8. Once you have completed one round, or the can is empty, ask everyone to reflect together on the experience of expressing needs. Ask:

    - *How did it feel to express a need?*

    - *Do you think it is OK to express a need?*

    - *What is it like to try to understand someone's need without judging the need?*

    - *What are we like as a family? Do we express needs? Do they get met? Are there a lot of unmet needs?*

9. Ask everyone to write their most urgent need on a note card.

10. Then ask each person to share that need with each member of the family.

11. Assign homework: Each family member should go home with their note card and write on the back of the card who could best meet their need and how they could ask. They should then ask the target person at least once to meet their need.

INTERVENTION 8

Many Hats

The Many Hats intervention asks family members to playfully take on different roles. These roles are represented by hats.

You will need: A variety of hats, such as a helmet, a simple cap, an elaborate hat with a feather, an improvised folded paper hat, a "Cat in The Hat" hat, a very large hat to "hide" under, etc. Note cards. Pencils.

Target Behavior/Emotion: Flexibility, recognition of needs/moods/roles.

1. Invite all present to participate in a playful activity about "wearing many different hats." Lay out the hats on the table or floor and ask everyone to sit in a circle.

2. Say: *We are all going to pick a hat and explain why we picked it.* Model this by picking a hat, let's say it's a fireman's helmet, and explain: *I picked this hat today because I feel like there is a lot going on and I will need to put out some fires in the family.*

3. Explain that there is not one specific right thing to say about each hat. Someone else might say this about the fireman's helmet: "I picked this helmet because it is red and red makes me happy. I need some happiness in my life today."

4. Explain that when the person who picked the hat talks, everyone else listens.

5. Now, ask the person next to you to begin. Go around the circle at least twice, as you want to reinforce the concepts of psychological flexibility and complexity. You can say: *Most people are more than one thing at a time and feel more than one feeling at a time.*

   Once you have gone around the circle twice, invite everyone to reflect about the exercise by asking the following questions (Also explain that family members should only talk about their own choice of hat):

   - *What did it feel like to wear these different hats?*

   - *Was this fun to do?*

   - *Is it OK to have fun in this family?*

   - *In real life, do you sometimes feel like you are always wearing the same hat, and would like to try a new one? Perhaps you don't want to put out family fires every day?*

   - *How would others in the family react if you chose a different hat?*

   - *Do you feel like you need a helmet a lot in your family?*

6. Pay attention to who is talking and how much. You may want to go around the circle to give everyone an opportunity to talk. Perhaps everyone could pick two questions to answer.

7. Once everyone has reflected about the exercise, give out note cards. Ask everyone to pick a hat they would like to wear for the following week.

8. Assign homework: Ask everyone to imagine wearing the hat they picked during a family event, meeting, or dinner. They should say something like: "Today I am wearing the big felt hat because I feel like I just need to hide right now." They should then observe what is different when they are wearing a different hat.

Put a Lid on It! Open the Lid

This intervention asks family members to attempt to symbolically put a lid on things, or take the lid off, if this is needed. As many families struggle with containing emotions, both individually and collectively, this intervention will help them sort: When is it necessary to put a lid on things? When is it necessary to open the lid?

You will need: A cooking pot with a lid is a useful prop, especially with children, but it's not necessary.

Target behaviors/emotions: Containment, affect regulation, communication.

1. Invite everyone to participate in an exercise about containment, communication, and expression and regulation of feelings.

2. Ask everyone to sit in a circle. Put the pot in the middle.

3. Ask for a volunteer to share an intense emotion. Ask the volunteer to describe the emotion in detail (but not so much that it would be traumatizing to others). You can give the following example:

   Sometimes I may be angry at someone, but I don't want to be. Or I think that the person does not deserve my anger. Or I think I should not be angry about this issue. Or I don't want to "blow up." Then I "put a lid on it."

4. Ask the volunteer to share the intense emotion and symbolically put it in the pot, then put a lid on it. Ask:

   - *What does this feel like?*

   - *Is it possible to put this feeling away?*

   - *Is the feeling now gone?*

   - *Can you retrieve the feeling?*

   - *What happens when the pot is on the stove and the lid is on tight?*

5. Now, ask every family member to contribute by talking about and exploring their intense emotions. Can they put a lid on it?

6. As you go around exploring everyone's emotions, look for how the family manages intense emotions. Do they always put a lid on it? Or do they always blow the lid off? When you detect a theme say: *It seems to me that in your family,* [insert the thing that you do you your family].

7. Ask everyone how the family's way of managing strong feelings works for them.

8. Explain that it is not always good to put a lid on a feeling, nor is it always good to blow the lid off. Explain that people, situations, and reactions can differ. You can illustrate this with the following story:

   There once was a toddler who was having a bad day. He wanted everything, but was not quite able to say so, and so he got nothing, at least not

what he wanted. Well, you can imagine how he blew his lid. He screamed,
and he cried, and he rolled on the floor.

Explain that this is what toddlers may do, but if you did this at work, it would probably not work out well for you. Ask: *Why is that?*

9. Help family members explore what they can say to each other to signal that they are struggling with containing a feeling. Something like this: *I feel like I am about to blow my lid. Can you help me?*

10. Also, identify what to say to each other when they feel like they need to put a lid on a feeling. Something like this: *Right now, I just have to put a lid on it. Can you help me?*

11. Explain that always putting a lid on it is unlikely to work in the long term. Always blowing up is also unlikely to work. But asking for help may just do the trick!

12. You could also work with the metaphor of turning the heat down. If the pot is on the stove, what would make the lid blow off? How does that work in this family? If one family member struggles with managing feelings, do others join and also become dysregulated? Is there a way to avoid this; in other words, to turn down the heat?

13. Ways of managing feelings can be divided along gender lines in families. Pay attention to this. Who always puts a lid on feelings?

14. Assign homework: Ask everyone to use and play with the phrases "put a lid on it" and "I need to take the lid off this one" for the following week to increase communication about feelings. Encourage everyone to ask for help when they struggle with intense feelings.

INTERVENTION 10

The Family Flag

This intervention asks your family to create a family flag. It asks the questions: What does this family stand for? How do we want to represent ourselves?

You will need: White fabric you can draw or paint on and pin things to. Fabric markers or paint. Colorful fabric pieces. Old magazines and glue. Scissors.

Target behaviors/emotions: Sense of community/connection/attachment. Recognizing differences and the whole. Acceptance. Negotiating.

1. Sit together at a table. If there is no table, you can sit on the floor. It's just easier to work at table.

2. Explain that you will be creating a family flag together. Brainstorm with the family:

   - *What do you want on the flag? What do you not want on the flag?*

   - *Are there any specific colors that represent your family?*

   - *Are there any specific objects that represent your family?*

3. Help family members recognize and respect differences in opinion. Keep a list of all suggestions. If there is an argument, just write down the suggestion and encourage everyone to move on. You are not making decisions yet, just brainstorming.

4. Once you are done brainstorming, ask everyone to pick two items from the list: something they personally feel strongly about including on the flag, and something that represents the family. If two people choose the same item, they get to work together to place the item on the flag.

5. Work together to design the flag on paper before decorating it. What will go where? This will then serve as a template for the flag.

6. Now, it is time to create the flag. Assign each family member a section of the flag. By now, each family member should know the design of the flag and where their item/color will go. Each family member should now paint or attach their chosen items on the flag. This can be a messy process. Take turns if needed and make sure everyone stays within the space assigned.

7. Remind everyone that things don't have to be perfect. This is especially important when children are participating. What matters is enjoying the process. It's OK if there is a feather sticking out on the side!

8. Help everyone reflect on the process of creating the family flag. You may want to use a second session. Ask the following questions:

   - *Do you like this flag?*

   - *What do you like about the family flag?*

   - *Was it fun to create the family flag? If yes, what was fun?*

   - *Was it stressful to create the family flag? If yes, what was stressful?*

- *In what way do you think this flag stands for your family?*

- *In what way does this flag not represent your family?*

- *Are there things on the flag that you don't want on it? If yes, can they be there anyway?*

- *How do you handle differences in the family? Is it OK to be different? To disagree?*

- *How do you negotiate when people don't agree?*

- *Do you think there can be a sense of unity in your family in spite of all the differences? How can this be built?*

9. Assign homework: Find a place in your home to display the family flag. Explore what you would like to add. Write these things on sticky notes and stick them next to the flag.

INTERVENTION 11

Gathering

In this intervention, family members gather three objects and use them to explore who they are and what is important for them. Objects can be gathered in the home or outside. If children are participating, they should, of course, not go outside alone.

You will need: Nothing specific. You just need to be in a place where there are objects to select from. If you are in an office setting, provide a basket of wildly different items.

Target Behavior/Skill: Communication. Meaning making.

1. Welcome everyone. Explain that today you will be learning more about each other using collected items. Give an example: Show an object and explain why it is meaningful to you and what it says about you. Here is an example:

    This is a sea shell. It is meaningful to me because I feel most at home by the ocean. When I am by the ocean, I feel connected. What does this say about me? I need to be in nature as much as possible to stay connected with what is important to me.

    Here is an example for a child:

    I brought this truck. I like it a lot because it rolls around and makes great sounds. I like this truck because I can play with it. What does this say about me? I love to play. When I play, I feel happy.

2. Instruct everyone to go and select three objects that are important or meaningful to them. No living or dead animals and the like. Tell everyone to take their time. This is not a race.

3. Smaller children should go with an adult. The child will get to pick their items first.

4. If it is possible, it is OK to go outside to pick items. But there are rules. Children cannot go outside alone and they must stay on the property.

5. If you are in an office setting, let people take turns taking items from a basket of things you keep in your office. You should have a basket of wildly different things in your office.

6. Give everyone 8–10 minutes to gather the items. You may want to ring a bell when time is up. Sometimes people get done a lot faster. This is OK.

7. Sit in a circle and explain ground rules: No interrupting. Once the person is done talking about the item, it is OK to ask a quick and friendly question, but it is not OK to criticize the item. Conversation about the item should be brief.

8. Ask the youngest person to begin by showing their first item. They should say:

    I brought this [item you brought].

> *It is meaningful to me (or I like it a lot) because* [what the item does for you/how it makes you feel/what it makes you think of].
>
> *What does this item say about me? It says that* [something important the item tells others about you].

9. Go around the circle until everyone has shown all three items.

10. Now, help all present reflect on what they have seen and heard by asking the following questions:
    - *Did you learn anything new about anyone?*
    - *What did it feel like to show your items? Were you nervous? Proud?*
    - *Were there any items that were similar?*
    - *How did you feel about listening to others?*
    - *Did you learn anything new about yourself?*
    - *Did you become impatient when listening to others? If you did, do you know why? How did you manage your impatience?*

11. Help everyone reflect on similarities and differences. Are there items everyone connects with? What about differences: Is it OK for family members to have wildly different interests?

12. Pay special attention to children. Ask: *Is it OK for children to have their own interests and make their own meanings? Or do we feel like we need to correct them?*

13. Ask everyone to put all of their items on the table. Say something like:

> *These are the things that are meaningful to people in this family. Some of them are alike. Some of them are not. Take a look at the great variety that makes your family who you are!*

14. Assign homework: Ask everyone to pick the item that is most important to them and talk with one family member about it over the next few days.

INTERVENTION 12

Going on a Trip

This intervention asks each family member to pick a destination they truly want to go to. They will describe this place in detail: What is special about it? What will they see and do? Who will be there? This will help family members connect about their relational wishes and a sense of adventure.

You will need: A list of questions about the destination to serve as prompts.

Target behaviors/emotions: Communication about relational wishes and a sense of belonging. Expression of needs and wants. Acknowledging differences.

1. Sit in a circle or around a table. Welcome everyone.

2. Explain that, today, every family member will get to "take a trip" by picking a destination and describing that place in detail. Here are some things they should explore:

    - What and where is this place?

    - How will they get there?

    - Will travel be dangerous?

    - What does the place look like? Is it in another country? What are the surroundings?

    - Is it warm or cold?

    - What would you like to do there?

    - Who is there with you?

    - How do you feel when you are there?

3. Invite the oldest family member to begin with their imaginary journey. Give this person the list of prompts and ask them to begin. Also explain to everyone that it is not OK to interrupt or belittle the speaker. It is OK to ask short and kind questions once the person is through.

4. When the first person seems to be finished, ask: *Are you all finished, or is there anything else you would like to say about this place?*

5. Then go around the room and ask everyone to explore their special place.

6. Once everyone has contributed, help them explore needs and wishes using the following questions?

    - *Do you think it is OK to dream?*

    - *In your family, is it OK to long for places and people far away?*

    - *When someone leaves, are they welcomed back? Or is there resentment that they left?*

    - *How similar are the places you are longing for? How different?*

    - *What happens in this family when people are tired of the same old thing? What do you do to "get away," or to create a change of scenery?*

- *In this family, is it OK to seek out new people?*
- *What would make you want to return home?*
- *What could you do to bring a little bit of that special place into your home?*

7. Once everyone has contributed, use this metaphor: *Everyone needs a nest and everyone needs wings.* Ask: *How can this family be a nest? How can this family allow everyone to use their wings?*

8. Assign homework: Ask each family member to identify one way in which they can bring an aspect of their special place into everyday family life.

INTERVENTION 13

Hurt Feelings

This intervention encourages all family members to acknowledge their emotional vulnerabilities. Additionally, family members will explore their willingness to ask for and accept support from others.

You will need: Items that symbolize "mending the hurt," such as band aids and bandages. If children are present, it is nice to bandage a teddy bear!

Target behaviors/emotions: Acknowledging vulnerability and hurt. Communication. Willingness to accept help and comfort.

1. Sit in a circle or around a table. Welcome all family members.

2. Explain that, today, you are going to explore together how people in the family experience and deal with emotional pain.

3. Begin by explaining the concept of emotional pain. If younger children are present, you can explain that a teddy bear has fallen and that his knee is bleeding. Take out the bandages and band aids and ask what should be done. Let the child help bandage the teddy bear, and ask what else could be done.

4. Explain that when feelings are hurt, this can be harder to spot, but there are some signs, such as crying, withdrawing, or displaying anger.

5. Ask everyone to imagine that the teddy bear's feelings are hurt. He is crying. Ask: *What could have happened? How do feelings get hurt? What hurts your feelings?*

6. Ask: *How do others know that your feelings are hurt? What do you usually do?* Say: *Here are the three basic options:*

    - *I become angry.*

    - *I keep it in and hide or get sad.*

    - *I use words to communicate about the hurt.*

7. Explain that most people do all of those things sometimes. Normalize the experiences of acting out, acting in, and communicating.

8. Explain that when feelings are hurt, words are often hard to find. This is especially true for smaller children, but really for all of us in the heat of the moment.

9. If children are present, take out the teddy bear. Ask everyone to say one thing to the teddy bear that could make things better when he is hurt.

10. If children are not present, ask participants to pair up and take turns saying this to each other: *When I am hurt, I* [the behavior you show when you are hurt].

11. Help the family reflect on how difficult it is to acknowledge hurt.

12. When everyone has contributed, ask the pairs to say this, taking turns: *When I am hurt, I would like you to help me by* [what you want the other person to do to help you].

13. Then help everyone reflect on how difficult it may be to ask for help. You can ask:

    - *In this family, is it OK to acknowledge hurt feelings?*

    - *What happens when someone acknowledges hurt feelings?*

    - *Do you rally together?*

    - *Do you try to avoid the hurt person?*

    - *Do you try to help? And if you do, how?*

14. Conclude by thanking everyone for being open about their hurt. Explain that hurt feelings can get in the way of meaningful connections in the family, and that it is better to address them. Sometimes people may need time to do so.

15. Assign homework: Ask everyone to identify their main style of expressing hurt. Then ask them to make a choice to do things differently. A person who usually withdraws and goes to their room should approach a family member and express their hurt.

INTERVENTION 14

Being a Pawn

This intervention gives participants the opportunity to experience what it feels like to be a pawn. What is it like to make your own moves? What do you feel like when someone moves you in a direction you do not want to go?

You will need: Stretched yarn to create to create an improvised race track.

Target behaviors/emotions: Frustration. Communication. Control. Letting go.

1. Begin by welcoming everyone. Then ask: *How many of you like it when someone tells you exactly what to do and you have no choice: you have to listen and do it?*

2. Invite participants to pair up: One person will be the pawn, the other will control the pawn.

3. Ask the pawns to line up at the starting point. Explain that the pawns will take one small step each time they fulfill a command from their controllers.

4. Ask the controllers to give orders that are difficult to follow, but not impossible (depending on the pawns' ages and developmental stages). An adult controller may ask an adult pawn to count backward from 100, or child pawn to count backward from 20. Here are some other ideas:

   - Fold an origami hat (you will need paper).
   - Stand on your left foot for three minutes.
   - Loudly sing "Row, Row, Row Your Boat" three times.
   - Draw a chicken.

5. You get the idea: The controller's role is to make things difficult for the pawn, who just wants to get to the finish line.

6. Let this game go on for at least 10 minutes. Perhaps someone will reach the finish line, though this is unlikely.

7. Now, ask everyone to stop and reflect on this exercise. Ask:

   - *What is it like to be a pawn?*
   - *What does it feel like to be constantly ordered around?*
   - *How frustrated were you?*
   - *What is it like to be a controller? Did you feel powerful?*
   - *What does power feel like?*
   - *Did you feel the pawn's frustration? If so, how did you respond to it?*

8. Now, help everyone reflect about control in the family. Ask:

   - *How does control work in your family?*
   - *Do you ever get frustrated because of all the rules?*
   - *What do you do when you feel stuck in this way?*

- *Why do you think people may become controlling?*

- *In what way does control work? In what way does it not work?*

9. Ask the adults: *What do you think it feels like to be controlled? What is your intention when controlling children?* You can say that, of course, there are legitimate reasons to control a child, such as keeping it from running into the street or touching a hotplate.

    Ask: *How can you make things less frustrating in the family? How can control be shared when possible? Are you willing to share?*

10. Assign homework: Ask each family member to practice letting go of controlling others when appropriate. For example, instead of ordering a child to clean her room, the parent could ask: "Do you want to clean your room now, or after dinner? What kind of help do you need with cleaning your room?"

INTERVENTION 15

Step by Step

This intervention will help family members acknowledge feelings of vulnerability and helplessness. It can be used when a family member struggles with such feelings and it is difficult for others to empathize.

You will need: Blindfold. A safe space to maneuver.

Target behaviors/emotions: Feelings of helplessness. Empathy.

1. Welcome everyone and explain that, today, you will explore feelings of helplessness and empathy together.

2. Begin by asking everyone to share feelings of helplessness. They could be related to a simple situation, such as losing car keys, or a larger issue, like a debilitating illness.

3. Ask everyone to share their responses to feelings of helplessness. If people struggle with this, they can pick from the following list and illustrate with examples:

   - I get angry and lash out at others.

   - I give up and just don't do anything.

   - I encourage myself.

   - I cry.

   - I ask for help.

   - I blame someone.

   - I think through the problem and try to solve it rationally.

   - I acknowledge that I feel helpless.

4. When everyone is done, provide psychoeducation about feelings of helplessness. You could say:

   Feeling helpless is a fundamental human experience. There are a lot of things we can do. There are also a lot of things we can't do. When we can't do something or control something, we naturally feel helpless. Recognizing this can guide us into more adaptive responses to helplessness, such as reaching out to others and problem solving. There are some problems that cannot be solved by just one person. There are also experiences of helplessness that can't be "fixed," such as when a loved one dies. These kinds of experiences are best addressed by supporting each other.

5. Invite participants to experience feelings of helplessness and empathy through an exercise.

6. Ask for a volunteer who will be blindfolded and will need everyone's help to maneuver from one place to another.

7. Explain ground rules:

- The blindfolded person can only take one small and careful step at a time.
- Those who guide the person must be helpful.
- Calm voices!

8. Blindfold the volunteer.

9. Designate a start and finish line for the exercise. There should be some obstacles in the way, such as a desk.

10. Now ask the family to direct the blindfolded person to the finish line, one step at a time, giving simple directions. No touching.

11. Family members should take turns giving directions.

12. Once the blindfolded person reaches the finish line, remove the blindfold.

13. Ask the blindfolded person to reflect on the experiences of helplessness and receiving help. You can use the following questions:
    - *How did you feel?*
    - *Were there times when you were scared?*
    - *Did you get frustrated or angry?*
    - *Did something funny happen?*
    - *Did you feel the help sometimes was not right?*

14. Then, ask the helpers to reflect on their experience of being helpers.
    - *How did you feel being a helper?*
    - *Did you get frustrated or angry?*
    - *Did you sometimes feel the blindfolded person did not respond correctly to your directions?*
    - *Were there moments when you wondered what if must feel like to be the blindfolded person?*
    - *Did you feel protective of the blindfolded person?*

15. Use the exercise to generally help family members reflect on experiences of helplessness. You can ask:
    - *What happens in this family when someone feels helpless?*
    - *Is it OK to acknowledge feelings of helplessness?*
    - *Who responds when someone feels helpless?*
    - *How do you solve problems in this family?*
    - *What do you do when a problem can't be solved?*
    - *How do you find out what the other person needs?*

16. Guide the conversation into the direction of empathy. You can say: *Even when a problem can't be solved, you can still there for the other person.*

17. Assign homework: Ask each family member to pick a partner and interview the partner about what they need when they feel helpless.

INTERVENTION 16

Mayday!

This intervention helps family members explore and understand what to do when the family is having the worst kind of day, when everyone is dysregulated and no one can fix it.

You will need: Poster board and marker.

Target Behavior/Emotions: Affect dysregulation, confusion, anger, rage. Family chaos. Restoring problem-solving.

1. Welcome everyone and explain that, today, you want to learn about the family's worst kind of day.

2. Ask for descriptions of the worst kind of day? What does this look like? What is the sound level? What kinds of things do people say? Explain that the purpose is information gathering, not blaming. Everyone should say "someone" instead of using names. Remind everyone that sometimes the best of people "lose it."

3. Ask the family to recreate the worst kind of day, at about 75% intensity. Insults should be toned down, and physical violence should only be described, not reenacted. Explain that the reenactment will be very short.

4. Once you have witnessed about 30 seconds of the reenactment, ask everyone to "freeze," and then return to their seats.

5. Ask: *How do you feel now?* Help everyone reflect on the intensity of feelings.

6. Develop a game plan for these kinds of days. Suggest that the first person who recognizes what is going on say, "Mayday." Take the poster board and label it: "What to do on a Mayday kind of day." When this happens, all family members should:

   - Create physical space between each other. Ask how this can be done and note it on the poster board.

   - Calm mind and body. Ask how each family member can do this, and make a note of it on the poster board.

   - Identify the problem from their point of view. Then make a note of this point of view on the poster board. Once calm is restored, family members should acknowledge that they may have different views of the problem.

   - Identify a day to address the problem. Explain that the kinds of problems that trigger a "Mayday" require some cooling-off time.

   - Identify a referee, a person who can help with problem solving, and note that on poster board.

7. Make a plan for a family conference to solve problems (note on poster board).

8. Explain that the poster board will go/stay home with the family so that they have it available when they need it. It should be kept in a location the family frequents often, such as the kitchen.

9. Assign homework: Ask each family member to identify problems or situations that make them feel like they need to say, "Mayday."

INTERVENTION 17

Retreat

This intervention helps the family recognize the need for building a retreat, a real or imaginary place of recovery troubles.

You will need: Imagination. Poster board. Marker.

Target behaviors/emotions: Emotional exhaustion. Recharging. Recovery. Self-care.

1. Welcome everyone and explain that, today, is a chance to design a place of recovery and self-care. Normalize the experience of needing to recharge after a difficult time.

2. Ask: *What do you do to recharge? Where do you go? What do you need?* Go around the room and ask everyone to describe their real or internal place of retreat. Explain that it can be real (such as a room) or internal (a state of mind).

3. Ask everyone to think about a family place of retreat. Explain that families, too, need to recharge. Families can become exhausted! Ask for specific examples of how the family could recharge together. You can use these questions:

   - *What gives all of you joy?*

   - *How could you relax together? What things do you need to relax together?*

   - *What activities could recharge you as a family?*

   - *What kind of space do you think you should be in together?*

   - *How much time is involved? How much planning?*

   - *Do you need to get any special items?*

   - *What could you do to express kindness to each other?*

4. While everyone is talking, take notes on the poster board. When the list is complete, ask the family to pick a time to hold the family retreat. Remind everyone to be realistic—tomorrow probably will not work.

5. Assign homework: Send the poster board home and ask everyone to pick one item from the list and prepare for the family retreat. Remind them that this is not a competition. It is not about who gets the best item for the retreat. It is about helping each other recharge.

INTERVENTION 18

The Mini Family Retreat

Being part of a family can be both wonderful and exhausting. By now, your family has learned how to plan for and schedule a family retreat to recharge. But there may not always be time to have a "full" family retreat. This intervention will help your family plan for mini retreats—little things family members will do for and with each other to recharge.

You will need: Imagination. Poster board. Marker.

Target behaviors/emotions: Emotional exhaustion. Recharging. Recovery. Self-care.

1. Welcome everyone. Ask about the family retreat. How did it go? What went well? Did they learn anything new about each other? Was it difficult to let go and simply recharge as a family?

2. Introduce the idea that families can build opportunities to recharge into each day and call this a mini retreat.

3. Explain that mini retreats are not time-consuming, and do not require a lot of effort. They can last a minute or two. For example: Before going to their separate rooms at night, family members could gather for a minute or two and reflect on what went well that day.

4. Brainstorm: Ask everyone to contribute to the list of things that can be done to create family mini retreats each day. Can they sit together for a cup of coffee in the morning? Listen to a song they all like? Divide a donut into pieces and share it? Pet the dog together? Look out the window and admire the clouds?

5. Remind everyone that mini retreats are not times to solve problems. They are for recharging.

6. Ask the family to schedule at least two mini retreats per day. Explain that, of course, it is OK to have more, and that no one should be rigid about missing a mini retreat. This just creates more stress. Sometimes not everyone can be present for every mini retreat. This is OK.

7. Assign homework: Ask your family to follow the mini retreat schedule for a week and give feedback at the next meeting. Explain that it is likely things will need to be tweaked.

INTERVENTION 19

What's on the Menu?

Any time people get together, things can get tricky. In families, it can be especially difficult for people to recognize and respect each other's likes and dislikes. This intervention will help family members recognize and respect their own and each other's likes and dislikes regarding relationships.

You will need: Paper and writing tools. Poster board and marker.

Target behaviors/emotions: Recognition of relational needs and preferences. Acceptance. Flexibility.

1. Welcome everyone. Explain that, today, you will explore family relationships together using the metaphor of a menu.

2. Begin by asking everyone to name their favorite foods. They should name a snack, a main dish, and a desert. Also ask them to describe what they like about each food.

3. Ground rules: Everyone must listen to each other. It's not OK to say "yuck" when someone else describes their favorite food, but it's OK to think it.

4. Once everyone has contributed (it's a good idea to go around the circle), help the family reflect by asking:

   - *Do you all like the same foods? Or are there differences?*

   - *Why do you think some people like some foods, and others do not? Is this OK?*

   - *Are there certain flavors almost everyone likes?*

   - *Are there certain flavors almost everyone dislikes?*

   - *Does it matter who makes the food?*

   - *Does it matter where it is eaten?*

   - *Do certain foods remind you of certain people in good and difficult ways?*

5. Explain that in family relationships, we can like or dislike different ways of relating, just like foods. Here is another way of saying this:

   In family relationships, things can get complicated, as each family member has likes and dislikes when it comes to relationships. In other words, what can be on the relationship menu for one person may not be on the relation-ships menu for another person. This does not mean that either one of them is wrong. It just means they like different things. If Joe likes to give hugs and Edwin hates to be hugged, neither one of them is wrong.

6. Explain that you will now create individual menus of relationship likes and dislikes. Give each person two pieces of paper and a pen. The first paper is for writing down what is definitely on the menu, relationally. The second paper is for writing down what is "off" the menu. These would be the kind of things that a person really dislikes. Give everyone some time to complete the menus. For most people, 5–7 minutes will be sufficient.

7. Go around the circle and ask everyone to go over their list, one by one. Remind everyone that respectful listening is the key. When someone has finished presenting their list, it is OK to ask respectful questions. It is not OK to belittle someone because of their relational likes and dislikes.

8. Now, ask the family to reflect together about individual likes and dislikes, using the following questions:

    - *Do you all like the same things relationally?*

    - *Or do you like different things?*

    - *Are there certain things almost everyone likes relationally?*

    - *Are there certain things almost everyone dislikes?*

    - *Are there conflicting relational likes and dislikes? If there are, name them clearly, without judgment.*

9. Conclude by saying:

    Today, you have learned from each other what you like and dislike in relationships. It can be difficult to listen without judgment. And yet, everyone has different ways of expressing themselves in relationships. Just recognize this for right now. People have different relationship menus, and this is OK.

10. Assign homework: Ask each family member to take home their relational menus and review them by asking themselves: "How flexible am I with each item? What is negotiable? What is not?"

INTERVENTION 20

The Family Menu

Just as individuals have certain relational likes and dislikes, so do families. Because in families individual relational likes and dislikes can be diverse and seemingly contradictory, the *Family Menu* of relational likes and dislikes will have to be negotiated. This intervention will help create a family menu of relational likes, something everyone can agree to engage in and enjoy.

You will need: Poster board and marker.

Target behaviors/emotions: Acceptance. Flexibility. Communication. Negotiating.

1. Welcome everyone. Remind everyone of the *"What's on the menu?"* intervention. Explain that, today, you will work together on creating a *Family Menu* of ways of relating.

2. Ask everyone to take out their homework from the last family session. Then go around the circle and ask each family member to present the revised list of what is definitely on the menu when it comes to ways of relating. Reiterate that now is the time for respectful listening.

3. Once everyone has contributed, take out the poster board. Explain that, now, you will create a family menu of relating together. Write *Family Menu* at the top of the poster board.

4. Then ask each family member to write their top two preferred ways of relating on the family menu. Here are some examples:

   - hugging
   - talking about it
   - friendly gaze
   - helping each other
   - taking a break together
   - taking a break alone
   - eating together
   - family conference
   - family game night
   - mending relationships
   - making things for each other
   - getting things for each other
   - telling it like it is
   - listening respectfully
   - accepting differences

You get the idea. Be sure that the list includes things that can be done that acknowledge difficulties in family relationships. Create opportunities to find answers to the question: What do we all like to do when things are tricky? Some families like to talk it out right away. Some need a break first. Both choices are OK.

5. Now, introduce the idea of a veto. Each family member can, but does not have to, veto one item on the list. Here is an example:

    Everyone but Jose likes hugs to show affection. This does not mean that hugs get taken off the menu. Rather, it means that the menu gets amended in the following way: Hugs are OK for everyone when there is consent, but not Jose. Just add this behind the menu item like this:

    Hugs (not Jose)

    Reiterate that there is nothing wrong with using your veto power. On the contrary: This helps all family members recognize each other's preferences.

6. Also explain that it is OK to make changes to the menu over time, just like restaurants do. So if, perchance, Jose begins to like hugs, he can cross out the exclusion of hugs.

7. Assign homework: Ask everyone to refer to the *Family Menu* when making relational choices. If new things need to be added to the menu, this is OK, but this has to be done collectively.

INTERVENTION 21

I Didn't Do It!

Taking responsibility can be difficult for everyone. In families, not taking responsibility can create resentment. When resentment builds, it can create rifts. This intervention will help all family members playfully address the "I didn't do it" experience—when no one did anything, and yet something went wrong.

You will need: Playfulness. Willingness to engage and assume goodwill by all family members. You will have to model and embody this. Poster board and marker.

Target Behavior/Emotion: Denial. Moving into acceptance. Communication. Problem solving. Empathy.

1. Begin by welcoming everyone. Explain that, today, you will explore the strange experience of things mysteriously going wrong. Here are some examples:

   - Toilet paper roll is always empty; does not get replaced.

   - Snacks are gone; no one ate them.

   - Feelings are hurt, but no one hurt them.

   - Things are missing, but no one took them.

   - Dirty dishes abound around the house, but no one used them.

   You get the idea. There are things in every family that go wrong, yet people have a difficult time taking responsibility for them.

2. Ask all family members what happens when they admit to something. You are trying to find out if the experience of admitting to doing something wrong is worse than the experience of denying responsibility. Listen to everyone. In most families, children will get scolded when they do something wrong. This can also happen between spouses.

3. Once everyone has explained what happens when they admit wrongdoing, ask the following questions:

   - *What would it feel like to admit to something, and not be scolded?*

   - *What would it feel like to admit to something if everyone had a sense of humor about things that went wrong that no one takes responsibility for?*

4. Ask everyone to engage in the following exercise. You will bring up a problem, then all family members, collectively, will say back to you: "I didn't do it." They can be very serious or funny about it.

   Go through all of the things that go wrong in this particular family. Here is what this would look like:

   You: There is no toilet paper again. Who did this?

   Family Chorus: I didn't do it.

   You: All the snacks are gone! Who took them?

   Family Chorus: I didn't do it!

You: You called me a piece of shit.

Family Chorus: I didn't do it.

You get the idea.

5. Now, help everyone reflect on what it felt like to deny responsibility for anything. You can ask:

    - *Did it feel like fun?*

    - *Did it feel like it solved the problem for you?*

    - *Did you feel guilty?*

    - *What did you think or feel about the person asking the question?*

    - *What about the toilet paper, the snacks, etc.? Are you ever bothered when things like this are missing or go wrong?*

6. Provide psychoeducation:

    Saying "I didn't do it" is often our first impulse. It is a way of pushing the problem away, of saying, "This has nothing to do with me," or even, "Don't bother me about this right now." So if someone, perhaps even you, responds to something by saying, "I didn't do it," even when they did or had some part in it, try to recognize this impulse. It is natural, but it can turn problematic when we can't move on from it. It may be a good idea to say: "Yep, I recognize this impulse to just say 'I didn't do it.'" Then move on to asking the questions that really matter:

    - *Is now a bad time to problem-solve about this?*

    - *Are you afraid I am going to scold or punish you harshly if you admit something?*

    - *Is there any chance you had any part in this? Perhaps just a little part?*

    - *Can you help me with this, anyway?*

    - *I am just trying to solve the problem. Do you have any idea of what we can do about this?*

    - *Are you feeling alone and abandoned because no one is admitting to this? How can I help you with that feeling?*

7. Ask each family to pick one of the questions from the preceding list that would be helpful for if they had done something wrong and had a hard time admitting it. Ask them to elaborate how the question would help them become more involved in problem-solving.

8. Create a list of helpful questions while family members are exploring this.

9. Assign homework: Send the list of questions home with the family and ask them to use it when "I didn't do it" situations come up.

INTERVENTION 22

I Didn't Mean It!

The "I didn't mean it" situation is a bit different. Someone in the family said something or did something that unintentionally caused some sort of harm or problem. This intervention will help family members explore new responses to unintentional harm. It will give everyone an opportunity to ask: What happened here? How did we respond? Is another response possible that will help all of us?

Please, note: This intervention is not meant to be used in families with a narcissistic manipulator who uses the phrase "I didn't mean it" to manipulate family members to excuse repeated and purposeful hurtful and harmful behavior.

You will need: Sense of humor. Willingness to reconsider (you will need to model and embody). Paper and writing tools. Poster board and marker.

Target Behavior/Emotion: Defensiveness. Flexibility. Communication. Moving on. Problem solving. Empathy. Perspective taking.

1. Welcome everyone. Inquire: Have you ever done or said something in the family that led to unintended consequences? Perhaps you felt completely misunderstood? Go around the circle and give everyone the opportunity to contribute.

2. Then ask: What did it feel like to be misunderstood or misinterpreted? Did you try to communicate the feeling? Go around the circle again.

3. If children are present, use developmentally appropriate words, such as: "When you knocked over the vase, did you mean to break it? Or was it an accident? When you got yelled at for knocking over the vase on purpose, how did you feel?"

4. Remind everyone to stick to the ground rules: Everyone should listen respectfully.

5. Now ask each family member to give an example of when they felt another family member did something problematic on purpose. Instruct them not to use names. Here is an example of what someone could say:

    The other day, someone shut the door right in my face. It really felt like they did this on purpose to get back at me. I felt awful, and I wanted to yell at them.

6. Ask everyone to notice, right now, that they have listened to the different sides of the problem:

    - *What does it feel like to be misunderstood?*

    - *What does it feel like to be hurt by someone who may not have intended it?*

7. Now, ask everyone to envision the following situation:

    Jose comes home after a tough day at school. Because he is frustrated, he does not pay attention when he walks in the house, and the door slams loudly. His mother storms toward the front of the house and yells: "Can't you ever be careful? You are always taking out your anger on me."

Jose mumbles something under his breath, something like, "I can't take this anymore." His mother becomes even more upset, and yells: "What do you mean? You can't take this anymore? You mean the free housing and food? The washing of your clothes? You are so ungrateful. You don't even know how good you have it." Jose turns to his mother and says: "Just shut up! I can't take it anymore!" He then walks to his room and closes the door. Jose's mom calls his dad and reports that Jose is mean and disrespectful, and will need punishment tonight.

8. Ask everyone:

    - *What went wrong here?*

    - *What is the first thing that went wrong?*

    - *What did Jose need from his mother when he came home?*

    - *What did his mother need from him?*

    - *What could Jose have said to make things better?*

    - *What could his mother have said to make things better?*

    - *Most importantly: Do you think Jose meant to hurt his mother when he came home and the door slammed?*

    - *What do you think would have happened if Jose had turned to his mother and said in a calm voice: "I didn't mean it. I am just frustrated with school. But not with you"?*

9. Divide family members into pairs and ask them to explore a situation in which one of them unintentionally caused a problem. Ask them to use the preceding questions. It might be helpful to write the above questions on a poster board or whiteboard. Of course, the name "Jose" can be replaced. Reiterate that the focus of this exploration is to uncover what is really needed and meant, as opposed to blaming the other person for what is happening.

10. Ask the pairs to report back. Then explore together how using the phrase, "I didn't mean it" or, "I didn't mean that" early could have changed the course of events.

11. Assign homework: Send home the poster board with the questions. Ask each family member to use those questions when they are assigning blame. Challenge everyone to ask:

    - "What happened? What was said and done?"

    - "Can I look at what happened another way?"

    - "Can I say: 'I did not mean it/that?'"

INTERVENTION 23

Me as a Tree

The tree metaphor helps with exploring how individuals relate to their families. They can be deeply rooted in ways that provide support, or they can be deeply rooted in ways that are not helpful. This intervention asks family members to explore how they are connected, using the tree metaphor.

You will need: Paper and drawing tools. It may be helpful to have a basic tree drawing handy, so clients can expand on this.

Figure 1

Target behaviors/emotions: Laying down roots. Acknowledging connections. Recognizing growth. Making change.

1.   Welcome everyone. Explain that they will engage in an art-based activity, drawing a tree, and that they will use the tree to explore family connection and disconnection, as well as ways in which changes are needed.

2.   Give each family member either a blank piece of paper or a tree image to expand on. Explain that the activity is not about how well they can draw, but, rather, to help everyone reflect about family.

3.   Ask everyone to begin by drawing a root system for themselves. Roots can be strong, weak, big, small, straight, twisted, whatever you'd like. Within these roots, ask everyone to draw or write the people, place, events, and things that have made them who they are today. Explain that these can be positive influences, such as a caring grandmother, or difficult influences, such as a family history of drug abuse.

4. If you are working with a foster family or any other family in which people have experienced a great deal of disconnection or disruption, explain that it is OK to have empty spaces. It is also OK to fill those spaces with things that are wanted or missed.

5. Then ask everyone to draw or write on the trunk of the tree who they feel they really are right now. Are they loving? Perhaps a good artist? Or do they feel stressed and overburdened? Perhaps someone is really meticulous? Explain that it is OK to make the trunk as big as it needs to be to make everything fit.

6. Next will be the top part of the tree. In this space, family members can draw whatever they would like. The top of the tree can be full, empty, growing, dying, whatever is appropriate.

7. Next, ask everyone to add branches to the tree. These will stand for ways in which each person wants to grow. An example would be a family member who would like to further their education or learn to connect better with others. Ask everyone to write or draw their growth wishes on the new branches.

8. Next, ask everyone to add leaves that are ready to fall off, and label them with things they no longer need in their lives, such as resentment, a hateful person, or a terrible memory.

9. Then ask everyone to draw the weather surrounding the tree. Is it sunny, cloudy, raining, or snowing? The weather happening around the tree describes the weather of life. Many families we work with have experienced an extraordinary amount of storms, and trees may be quite bent.

10. Last, is there anything around your tree? Ask family members to add to the surroundings. They can add things like friends or activities.

11. Once everyone has finished, go around the circle and ask them to share three things about their tree drawings that they find important. Remind everyone to listen and speak respectfully.

12. Once everyone has contributed, help everyone reflect about themselves and their family. Ask the following questions:

    - *In what way are the drawings alike?*
    - *In what way are they different?*
    - *Are there things everyone is happy about?*
    - *Are there things everyone is bothered by?*
    - *In what way are family roots helpful? In what way are they not?*
    - *In this family, is it OK to grow new branches?*
    - *In this family, is it OK to let go of some leaves?*

13. Assign homework: Ask the family to post all drawings together on a wall at home and ask each other questions about their trees. Also explain that it is OK to not answer questions that are not comfortable.

INTERVENTION 24

Amplify!

There is often one person (or more) in the family who feels that they do not have a voice. There could be many reasons for this. Families can get stuck in their ways of communicating. This intervention is designed to get the family unstuck in a specific way: By amplifying the voices of the least heard.

You will need: Real or toy microphone.

Target behaviors/emotions: Communication. Listening. Having a voice. Courage.

1. Welcome everyone. Explain that, today, you will amplify the voice of the person(s) who feels the least heard in the family. Explain that, frequently, this person has a lot to contribute.

2. Say: *It is important to listen to this person, not just because they need to be heard, but because the family would miss out on this person's contributions.*

3. Explain that there can be more than one person whose voice needs to be amplified. Also explain that this intervention is not for those who speak up a lot but feel misunderstood. It is for those who rarely speak up, whose voices are drowned out.

4. Determining whose voice needs to be amplified is the hard part. That person is the least likely to say so. Ask family members to look around the room and ask themselves the following questions:

   - Who do I tend to forget about?

   - Who do I rarely see?

   - Who just "shuts up" when there is trouble?

   - Who never engages in an argument?

5. Using these questions, explore together who should get a chance to use the microphone. Keep in mind that this will not be easy for the person whose voice needs to be amplified.

6. Once the family has made a choice, go around the circle and ask each family member to finish this sentence:

   I want to hear from you because [the reason that you think the identified person has important things to say].

7. Give the chosen person the microphone and a copy of the following prompts and ask her to finish each sentence:

Here is what I have always wanted to say
It can be difficult for me to speak because
When there is trouble, I feel
Because I am a quiet person, I
When everyone talks, I
What would be really helpful for this family would be
If I could change one thing about us as a family, it would be
Anything else the person wants to say (that is respectful)

Figure 2

8. Remind everyone to listen respectfully. In this case, there are no interruptions allowed. Also, ask everyone to give this person time to think about her words. This means that everyone has to have patience. Just because someone is thinking does not mean this person is done talking.

9. When the person is all done, they should say, "That is all" to signal that they are done.

10. Now, help everyone reflect on what they just heard, using the following questions:

    - *Did you learn anything new about this person?*
    - *Did you learn anything new about your family?*
    - *Is there anything you should do or change, based on what you just heard?*

    Please, note that this is not a "free-for-all" discussion. No attacking the person whose voice was amplified. This person needs to be protected.

11. Assign homework: Ask everyone to take some time to listen with care to the person who spoke today. This can be done by asking them a question or simply making sure that when they speak, they get a chance to be heard. Sometimes it can be helpful to send a toy microphone home to help with the listening process.

Helping Hands

This intervention invites everyone to think about the ways the family needs and receives help. Many families have one outside person who comes to the rescue when needed. Family members will explore in what ways this person is helpful and how they themselves can become helpers within the family.

You will need: Paper and writing tools. Two poster board and marker. Ribbons and tape.

Target behaviors/emotions: Helplessness and help-seeking. Empowerment. Recognition of abilities.

1. Welcome everyone. Explain that, today, you will explore together in what ways the family needs help and who comes to the rescue.

2. Ask everyone to tell a story about when the family needed help. Take out a poster board with the following questions and read them out loud:

   - What was the situation that required help?

   - Who came to help?

   - Has that person helped before?

   - Was that person helpful?

   - If they were, what did they do or say?

   - What kinds of characteristics does this person have?

   - Is there anything you admire about this person?

3. Once everyone has contributed, ask the following questions:

   - *Is it OK that this family sometimes needs help?*

   - *What does it mean that we sometimes need help?*

4. Help everyone explore in more detail what makes the family helper so helpful. Identify specific ways in which the helper helps or specific qualities the helper possesses. To do so, first, determine: Who is the person who helps the most? Then, take out the second poster board and dig deeper about this person by asking everyone to answer the following questions:

   - How is this person with you when they help? What does this person say or do? How do they look at you? How kind are they?

   - Are they very practical?

   - Does this person have resources, such as time or money?

   - Is this person a good organizer?

   - Are they friendly? Do they genuinely care about the family?

   Note the family's answers on the poster board.

5. Next, circle the most important things this person does. Ask the family to determine what those things are.

6. Let's say there are four really important things about this person. Here is an example:

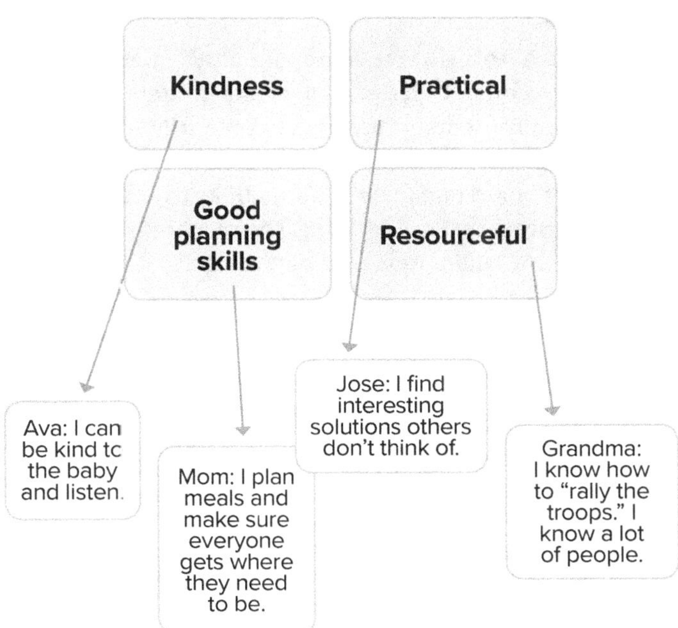

Figure 3

7. Next, go around the circle and ask everyone to match themselves with the square that closest fits them, and explain why. This does not have to be an exact match. You don't have to be kind all the time to match yourself with the kindness square, you just have to have the capacity to be kind.

8. Once this is completed, ask everyone what the most common family crisis is. When does the family most need help?

9. Then, ask everyone to apply their special skill to the situation. Ask:

    - *How could you use your special skill to help, even if you can't solve the problem?*

    - *What, specifically, could you do?*

    - *How can you rely more on each other?*

10. Explain that it is always OK to ask for help when needed, but that you are confident that this family has skills to address problems. Again, explain: You are not looking for perfection. But what would happen if everyone used their special skill just a bit?

11. It may be fun to write the special skills on ribbons and award each family member.

12. Assign homework: Ask family members to practice their special skills.

INTERVENTION 26

Warring Fractions

It is normal for alliances to form within families. But sometimes those alliances lead to battles. This intervention is designed to create awareness of alliances and the functions they serve. Family members are then temporarily "reassigned" to alliances they are not normally part of.

You will need: Poster board and marker. Your ability to embody calm.

Target behaviors/emotions: Scapegoating. Overgeneralizing. Dehumanizing. Assigning blame. Empathy. Willingness to allow change.

1. Welcome everyone. Begin with psychoeducation. Explain that any time humans come together, it is likely that they will form alliances. There is nothing wrong with people supporting each other. Things can become tricky when an "us-versus-them" situation develops.

2. To help everyone understand "us-versus-them" situations, help the family name and explore situation outside of the family in which people form groups and stand in opposition to each other.

3. Explore those alliances. What do they do for the people who are part of them? You can always use the example of sports teams. Why do people rally around a team? How do they feel when they rally for their team with others?

4. On poster board, create a list of positive things that happen when people form alliances.

5. Then, go around and ask everyone: *Have you ever felt excluded from a group or team? What happened that made you feel excluded? How did people treat you differently because you were not a part of their team or group? Did you feel hurt? If so, why?*

6. On another poster board, create a list of negative effects of an "us-versus-them" situation.

7. Next, help family members explore and understand how they form alliances in the family, how these alliances are helpful, and how they can cause hurt. You can use a poster board to illustrate this. Here is what this may look like:

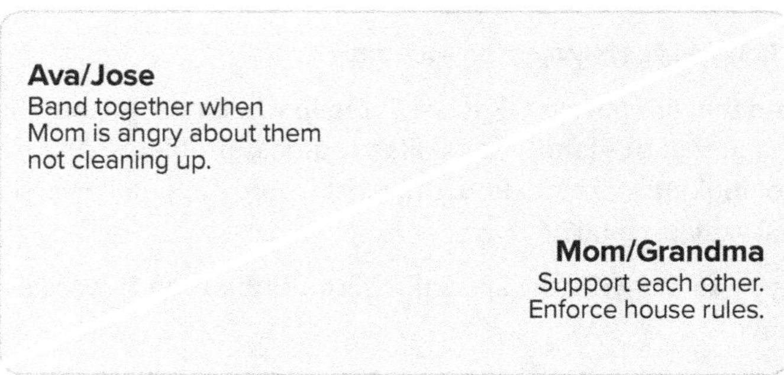

Figure 4: Example of a helpful alliance.

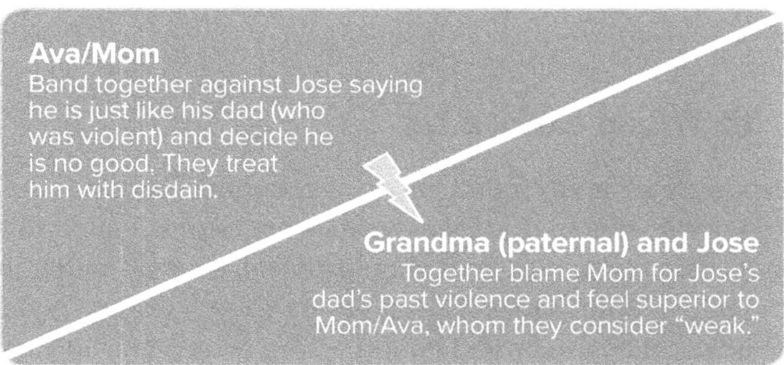

Figure 5: Example of an alliance than can result in more hurt.

8. Now, propose an experiment: Ask family members to put themselves in the shoes of another person with whom they normally are not aligned. Explain that this is not the time to be hurtful. They should truly attempt to understand what that other person really needs by pretending to be that person and completing the following sentences:

    I am [family member you are portraying]. *What I really need is* [what you think that family member needs].

    I need others in the family to [identify one thing that you think the family member really wants the family to do].

    I feel hurt when [what you think really hurts that family member].

    I feel included when [things the family member would like to be included in].

9. Once everyone has been "on the other team," help everyone reflect on what it is like to pretend to be the other person.

10. Explain that the goal is to help everyone understand that those who are on the other team are also humans and need respect. They are also a part of the family.

11. Assign homework: Ask everyone to spend time with someone in the family they usually do not align with. Explain that it is important to do fun things together. Part of the task is to identify something both enjoy, and then do it.

INTERVENTION 27

Walking with Those Before Us

This intervention asks family members to make connections with their ancestors. (If you are working with children, explain what an ancestor is.) Ancestors can be powerful supporters. They can teach us about survival, courage, and humor. They can also remind us of painful family histories that we don't want to repeat. This intervention should not be used with families whose members who struggle with psychosis.

You will need: It is nice, but not necessary, for people to bring photos of their favorite or most meaningful ancestor. If you would like family members to do this, you should ask them to look for photos several weeks in advance. Paper and pencils. Relaxation music.

Target behaviors/emotions: Making connections. Acknowledging the past. Taking Courage. Mindfulness.

1. Welcome everyone. Explain that, today, you will explore connections with important family members who are no longer with us. Explain that it is also OK to include family members, living or deceased, who are important but out of reach. This can be especially helpful when you are working with foster children.

2. Be mindful that painful feelings of loss can come up during this intervention. This is OK. You can say things like:

    Your sadness is a testimony to the love between you and [the person who died].

    It's OK to miss someone who you were close to.

    Clearly, this person had a great impact on you. Today we are thinking about how this impact can continue.

3. Ask everyone to take a moment to think about an influential person, either deceased or out of reach. Give them a piece of paper and ask them to write down the name of the person as well as why this person was so important. Give everyone a few minutes to complete this.

4. When everyone is finished, ask all family members to bring their person into the room by naming them and explaining why they were, and still are, so important. Sometimes children may choose a living and present person. This is OK.

5. Once everyone has introduced their person, ask:

    - *What is it like to bring this person into the room?*

    - *What feelings came up?*

    - *Is it OK to miss someone?*

Help everyone reflect on these questions together.

6. Next, ask everyone to get up and begin walking in a circle together. Say: *You are now walking together as a family.*

7. As you are walking together, ask each person to imagine that the person they chose is walking next to them. You can say something like this:

    Image that ______________ is walking right next to you. She/He is with you in many ways. She reminds you, she guides you, she makes you smile and she helps you get through. She says: Keep on walking. I am beside you.

8. Keep walking for a couple of minutes. It can be helpful to play relaxation music.

9. Ask everyone to reflect on the experience of walking together as a family and walking with their person.

10. Assign homework: Ask everyone to identify helpful ways in which they can connect with their important person, even if that person is deceased or absent.

INTERVENTION 28

Moving Toward the Light

Many families we work with have an intense focus on interpersonal problems. When we walk in the door, the first thing we often hear are complaints about family members, often children. Perhaps they were disrespectful or hurtful or they did not do well completing a task. It is tempting, and sometimes necessary, to begin each meeting exploring the unfortunate events of the prior week.

This intervention asks both the provider and the family to do the opposite: To "tilt toward the light" in the face of all that has gone wrong in the family; in other words, to move toward interactions that bring joy and satisfaction into each other's lives.

You will need: A room with a window or a lamp that radiates warm light, such as a salt lamp.

Target behaviors/emotions: Doing what works. Flexibility. Acceptance. Mindful presence. Joy.

1. Welcome everyone. Begin with this story:

   Jose is a third grader and he is bringing home his quarterly report card. He is doing fine. All of his grades are acceptable, except for his math grade. It is a C. There is also a brief remark on his report card about Jose speaking out of turn.

   Jose's mother immediately begins questioning him about his C in math and his behavior. Jose becomes agitated and begins to cry, then yell. Jose's mother is also upset, and says loudly: "I don't know what I am going to do with you. I just don't know."

2. Ask everyone to reflect on what happened with Jose and his mother. Mention that all of his grades are OK and that he is not failing math.

3. Explain that we often tend to focus on the one thing that goes wrong, even when many other things are going well.

4. Ask for examples from family members. When have they focused on negatives right away? When has someone else focused on negatives in their interactions? Remind everyone that this is a time for respectful listening and speaking, not personal attacks.

5. Provide reassurance for everyone by saying this: *It is natural to focus on all that goes wrong. It's what our brains do to make sure that we are safe. If something goes wrong, we want to address it right away. This is a natural impulse. However, this impulse can be unhelpful. What happened to Jose and his mother? How are they both feeling? What is happening in their relationship?*

6. Ask everyone to move into the darkest corner of the room. Ask: *What does it feel like to stand there together?*

7. Next, ask everyone to walk over to the window, paying attention to each other and letting children stand in front so they can look outside. Ask: *What*

does it feel like to stand here together? How much more do you see? Can you feel the sun?

8. Have everyone sit down again. Go around and ask everyone:

    - *What could you do as a family to move toward the light?*

    - *What could you as an individual do to recognize and focus on what is going well?*

9. Explain that you are not asking family members to ignore problems, but, rather, to focus first on what is generally going well. The instruction for everyone is to "Move (or at least tilt) toward the light." You may want to give out laminated index cards with this phrase that can be carried around because the impulse to focus on negatives first can be so strong.

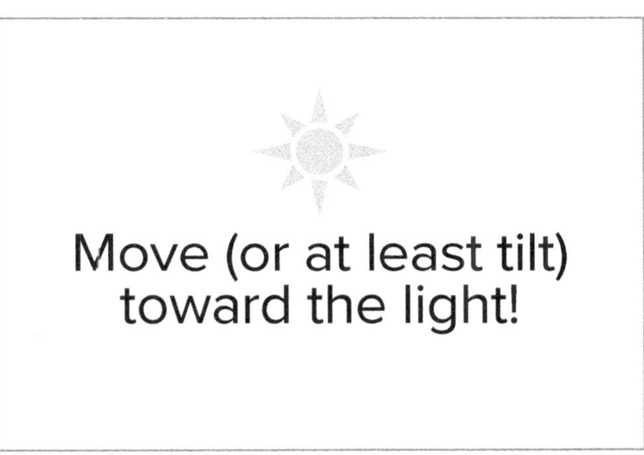

Figure 6

10. Assign homework: Ask everyone to look for "turnaround moments" in the family every day. A turnaround moment is a moment that could shift into a focus on negatives, but that can be turned around into focusing on what is going well. Explain that parents and caretakers are instrumental in making this work. Children will follow if adults take the lead.

INTERVENTION 29

Musical Chairs

This intervention brings to the forefront the emotional hurt that stems from competition and exclusion in families. At first glance Musical Chairs seems like a fun game. Everyone rushes to get a chair. This can result in an amusing chaos. However, the game is really "rigged" against those with processing and emotional difficulties. If you can't process fast enough, you will be "out" quickly. You are then likely to experience the feelings of failure and exclusion—something you are probably already familiar with. This intervention asks family members to listen to the voices of the excluded and find a new way of playing musical chairs, one that is inclusive and honors difference, rather than punishing it.

You will need: A row of chairs or pillows, though the latter may be difficult for those with physical limitations. Music.

Target Behavior/Emotions: Competitiveness. Hurt feelings. Acceptance. Valuing difference. Creating joy.

1. Welcome everyone. Explain that, today, you will begin with an experiment: you will engage in Musical Chairs together. Explain the game, if necessary.

2. Ask everyone to help you line up the chairs.

3. Establish ground rules: No shoving, pulling, hitting, etc. It's OK to be quick. It's not OK to hurt anyone.

4. Start the game. After the first round, ask the person who did not make it to a seat to stand with you. If this person is upset, explain quietly that in this case, Musical Chairs is not about "winning," and that everyone will find out soon.

5. After the second round, ask everyone to put the chairs back into a circle. You could also sit at a table together.

6. Explain that you are not going to continue until there is a winner, but, rather, that you are going to reflect together on the experience of exclusion and losing.

7. Ask the two people who are "out" to answer the following questions:

   - *How are you feeling about being "out" or "losing"?*

   - *Does this happen to you a lot?*

   - *Do you feel that Musical Chairs is a fair game for you to engage in?*

   - *What are your strengths?*

   - *What are your weaknesses, and how do those weaknesses affect your ability to "win" in Musical Chairs?*

8. Now, ask everyone to reflect on Musical Chairs and the impact this activity can have on family members, using the following questions:

   - *How would you feel if you were constantly losing or out first?*

- *Would you want to engage in Musical Chairs if you had trouble concentrating?*

- *Would you want to engage in Musical Chairs if you often felt sad or angry?*

- *Would you want to engage in Musical Chairs if you already felt lonely or unappreciated in the family?*

9. Help everyone reflect on the "how come" of their answers.

10. Often, there is someone who will say something like this: "Life is tough, and you have to live with that. If you lose, you just have to be tough and take it." If this comes up, explore the idea of the family being a "nest," a sort of refuge from all the competitiveness of life. In your family, you learn acceptance and are valued for who you are, with all of your wonderful and tricky aspects. The experience of acceptance in the family is what prepares you to manage difficult experiences outside of the family. You cannot learn to manage difficult experiences without the experience of acceptance.

11. Ask everyone to re-design Musical Chairs. How could they engage in this activity without creating experiences of emotional hurt, rejection, or loss?

    Here are some ideas:

    - Ask the youngest person to suggest an animal. Play a song. During the song, everyone acts like that animal. When the song stops, the next person gets to pick an animal, and so forth.

    - Ask the youngest person for their favorite song and play it. Everyone should imitate the movements of the person who chose the song. When the song stops, the next person gets to pick a song, and so forth.

    Be sure that whatever your family comes up with, it is not competitive.

    If there is a family member with autism who is bothered by loud sounds, you can eliminate the sound and go with just movement and gestures.

12. Once you have engaged in the new version of Musical Chairs, ask everyone to reflect using the following questions:

    - *How do you feel now?*

    - *Was this experience fun? In what way?*

    - *Did your feelings get hurt this time?*

    - *Was there anyone who made you laugh?*

    - *How do you feel as a family after this activity?*

13. Assign homework: Ask the family to pick a time to engage in the new activity together!

INTERVENTION 30

From: Not Us! To: Us!

This intervention helps families explore and understand negative ways in which dominant culture may have affected them. The family will ask together: "Is this really what we believe? Is this really how we do things? Or are we just doing what is 'out there'? If there are ways in which the habits of dominant culture of dominant culture are hurting our family, how do we want to change these habits?"

You will need: Poster board. Marker.

Target behaviors/emotions: Identifying family values. Acceptance. Valuing difference. Recognizing connection.

1.   Welcome everyone. Explain that, today, you will explore together how the family may be affected by outside pressures. You may want to give an example like this:

     We are often told that we must always do better and do more. But I am wondering if always doing better and more is a good message to give to children, when it comes to family. How can we give everyone in the family the message that they are "good enough" and are loved and valued just as they are?

2.   Take out the poster board. Draw a line in the middle and label the two sections like this:

Dominant Culture Values/Messages	Us
Examples: Get more stuff Do what you have to do	Examples: Spend more time together Take care of each other

Figure 7

3. Go around the circle and ask everyone to identify dominant culture messages. You may have to dig deep. Often, families have absorbed dominant culture messages they do not really believe in. Help your family question those values. You can ask questions like this:

   - *When it comes to "every man/woman/child for himself/herself", what does this mean for Grandma Ida, who has dementia? Or Jose, who has a developmental disability?*

   - *Does more stuff really make you happy? Have you noticed that when you get more stuff, you often want even more stuff?*

   - *Do you ever feel that dominant culture has hurt you as a family?*

   - *In what way are you already different as a family and happy about it?*

4. Then ask everyone to identify "us" messages. These are the values that make this family what it is. Help everyone reflect on the "us" messages by asking the following questions:

   - *If you lived these values every day, how would your lives be different?*

   - *Is there a way to integrate your values more into your everyday lives?*

   - *How can you pass on your values to your children? How can you "be" your values?*

5. Assign homework: Create a value calendar for the week. Ask everyone to incorporate the value of the day. Here is a value calendar to use; this can be posted on the fridge or above the kitchen table:

Family Value of the Day	
Day	**What I will do today to bring this value to life**
Mon	
Tue	
Wed	
Thu	
Fri	
Sat	
Sun	

Figure 8

Appendix: Selected Figures

Figure 1

Here is what I have always wanted to say
It can be difficult for me to speak because
When there is trouble, I feel
Because I am a quiet person, I
When everyone talks, I
What would be really helpful for this family would be
If I could change one thing about us as a family, it would be
Anything else the person wants to say (that is respectful)

Figure 2

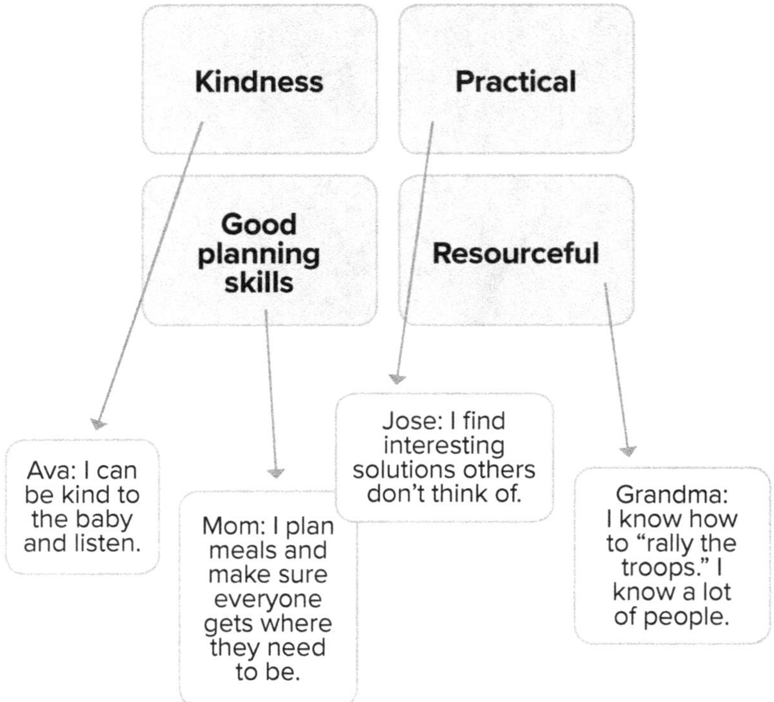

Figure 3

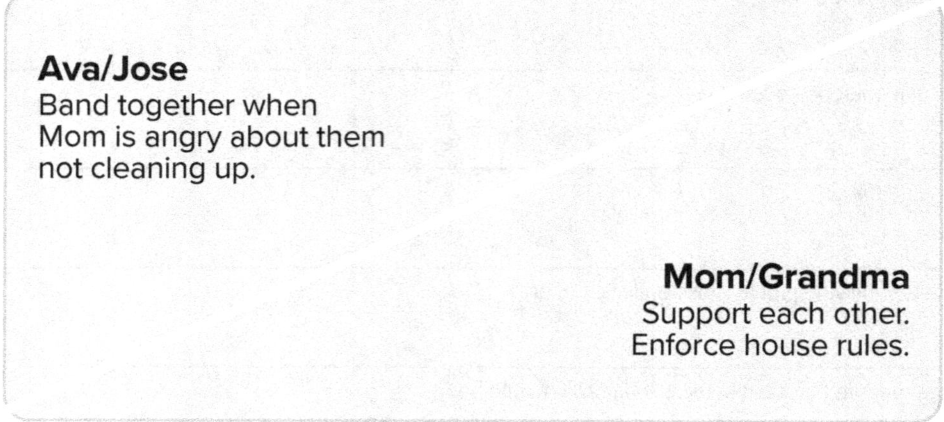

Figure 4: Example of a helpful alliance.

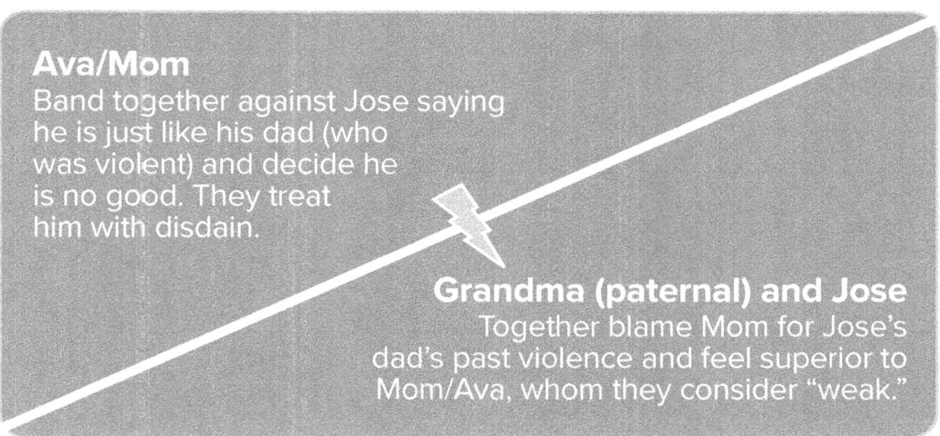

Figure 5: Example of an alliance than can result in more hurt.

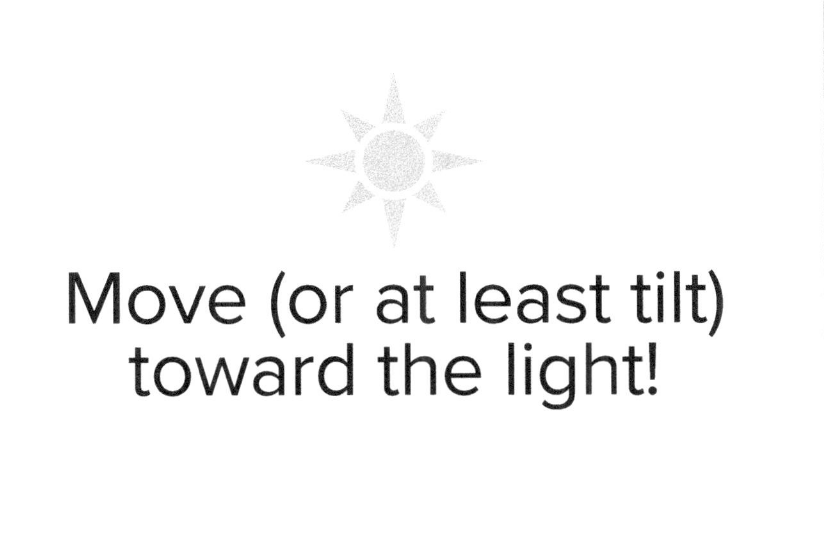

Figure 6

Family Value of the Day	
Day	**What I will do today to bring this value to life**
Mon	
Tue	
Wed	
Thu	
Fri	
Sat	
Sun	

Figure 8

Bibliography

Nichols, M. P., & Davis, S. D. (2017). *Family therapy: Concepts and methods.* Boston, MA: Pearson.

McGoldrick, M. (2011). *The genogram journey: Reconnecting with your family.* New York, NY: W.W. Norton & Co., Inc.

http://multiculturalfamily.org/